Grades 0–1

Improve your sight-reading! duets

Paul Harris

Contents

FABER 𝆑𝆑 MUSIC

Can be used alongside
Improve your sight-reading!
Pre-Grade 1, Stages 1–4

Pre-Grade 1 Stage 1

1 **Cup of tea**

Bouncing

2 **By the lake on a warm summer's day**

Floating

3 **March of the piano teachers**

With energy

© 2012 by Faber Music Ltd

Pre-Grade 1 Stage 1

1 Cup of tea

1 How many times is the pattern in bar 1 repeated?
2 How many differences can you find between bar 1 and bar 3?

2 By the lake on a warm summer's day

1 How many beats will you count for each note in bar 1?
2 Which hand will you use (which clef is used)?

3 March of the piano teachers

1 Are bars 1–4 similar in any way to bars 5–8?
2 Clap or tap the rhythm.

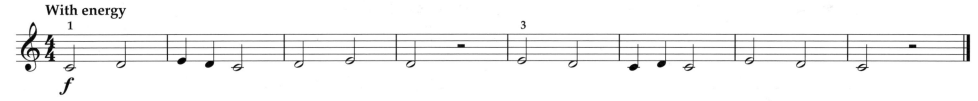

Pre-Grade 1 **Stage 2**

Can be used alongside
Improve your sight-reading!
Pre-Grade 1, Stage 5

1

A couple of aliens pop in for breakfast

Crisp and Martian-like

2

Who's that knocking at the door?

Heavily

3

What's the time?

Like clockwork

Pre-Grade 1 Stage 2

1

A couple of aliens pop in for breakfast

1 How many beats will you count for the D in bar 4?
2 How many examples can you find of repeated notes?

Crisp and Martian-like

2

Who's that knocking at the door?

1 Can you find any differences between bars 1–4 and bars 5–8?
2 How will you bring this piece to life? Who is knocking at the door?

Heavily

3

What's the time?

1 What do you notice about the rhythm in bars 1, 2, 4, 5, 6 and 8?
2 Name the letter names of all the notes in bar 3.

Like clockwork

Can be used alongside
Improve your sight-reading!
Pre-Grade 1, Stages 6–8

Pre-Grade 1 Stage 3

1 **By a cool mountain stream**

Gently flowing

2 **Tango to take away**

With a Spanish flavour

3 **I missed my lesson**

Very sadly

Pre-Grade 1 Stage 3

More intervals

1 **By a cool mountain stream**

1 How many different rhythmic patterns can you find in this piece?
2 How will you bring out the character?

2 **Tango to take away**

1 Compare bars 1–2 with bars 5–6.
2 Clap the rhythm of the piece while counting the pulse.

3 **I missed my lesson**

1 What is the letter name of the first note? Are there more examples of that note?
2 Clap the rhythm of the piece then hear the rhythm in your head.

* We haven't done accents yet, but they would sound good here!

Pre-Grade 1 **Stage 4**

1   The bell ringers' tea party

1 To which scale do the first five notes belong?
2 Play the first note then try to hear the piece in your head.

Like the sound of ringing bells

Hold down the sustaining pedal (on the right!) throughout this piece if you like.

2   Ice cool

1 In which key is this piece?
2 How many repeated patterns can you find (melodic and rhythmic)?

Lightly

3   A ceremonial affair

1 What interval is formed by the 3rd and 4th notes of bar 1?
2 Is any bar repeated?

Gracious and broad

Pre-Grade 1 **Stage 4**

Can be used alongside
Improve your sight-reading!
Pre-Grade 1, Stage 9

1

The bell ringers' tea party

Like the sound of ringing bells

2

Ice cool

Swing lightly

3

A ceremonial affair

Gracious and broad

Pre-Grade 1 **Stage 5**

Can be used alongside
Improve your sight-reading!
Pre-Grade 1, Stage 10

1 **Lazing around on a Saturday afternoon**

Slowly, without energy

2 **Chugging along nicely**

Chugging along

3 **It's as easy as one, two, three** ...

Allegretto

Pre-Grade 1 **Stage 5**

1 **Lazing around on a Saturday afternoon**

1 Are there any similarities between the right- and left-hand passages?
2 Clap or tap the rhythm of the piece.

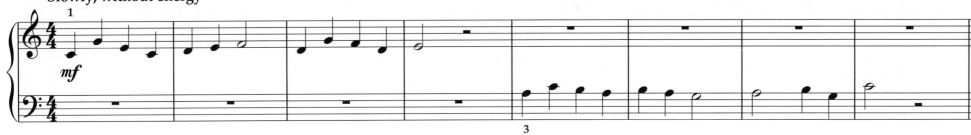

2 **Chugging along nicely**

1 What is the interval between the first two notes? Does this interval occur again?
2 Tap the pulse and hear the rhythm of the piece in your head.

3 **It's as easy as one, two, three ...**

1 Bar 2 doesn't follow the general pattern. Why?
2 Play the first note and try to hear the piece in your head.

Pre-Grade 1 **Stage 6**

Can be used alongside
Improve your sight-reading!
Pre-Grade 1, Stage 11

1 □ **Waltz of the elegant piano lid**

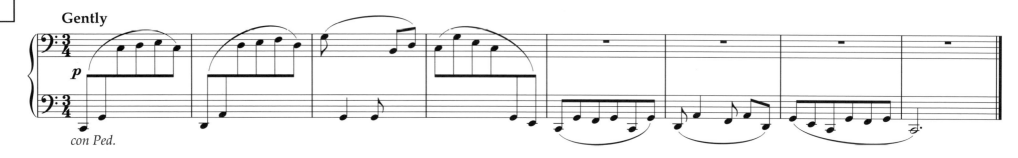

2 □ **Can't get a signal on my mobile**

3 □ **Dance of the hammer and the nail**

Pre-Grade 1 **Stage 6**

¾ 𝅗𝅥.

1 **Waltz of the elegant piano lid**

1 How many beats are there in each bar? What will you count?
2 Clap or tap the rhythm, counting the pulse carefully.

2 **Can't get a signal on my mobile**

1 Clap or tap the rhythm, then hear the rhythm in your head.
2 What do we call the pattern formed by the first three notes in the right hand?

3 **Dance of the hammer and the nail**

1 How will you give character to this piece?
2 Clap or tap the pulse and hear the rhythm in your head.

Grade 1 Stage 1

Can be used alongside
Improve your sight-reading!
Grade 1, Stages 1–3

1 **Strolling down the lane without a care in the world**

Dreamily

2 **I'll have a Spanish omelette (with chips)**

With castanets

3 **Ben's boogie**

Boogie tempo

Grade 1 Stage 1

1 **Strolling down the lane without a care in the world**

1 In which key is this piece? Play the scale (or micro-scale).
2 Tap the rhythm of the piece whilst counting the pulse. Now hear the rhythm in your head.

2 **I'll have a Spanish omelette (with chips)**

1 What interval is formed by the first two notes? Does it occur again?
2 Tap the rhythm of the piece whilst counting the pulse. Now hear the rhythm in your head.

3 **Ben's boogie**

1 What pattern is formed by the first three notes? Does it occur again?
2 What does the symbol in the last bar mean?

Can be used alongside
Improve your sight-reading!
Grade 1, Stage 4

Grade 1 Stage 2

1
Blowing hot and cold

Flowing gently

2
Smooth piece

Lazily and very smoothly

3
Dancing a habanera after a delicious paella

With spirit

Grade 1 Stage 2

1

Blowing hot and cold

1 Clap the rhythm, observing the dynamic levels.
2 How will the phrase marks affect your performance?

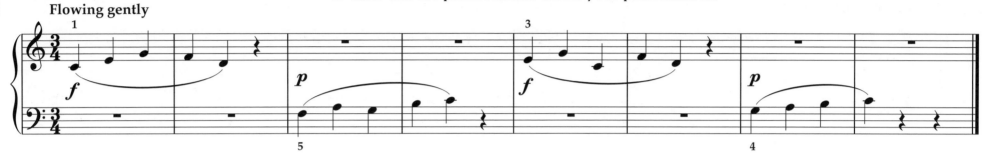

2

Smooth piece

1 Can you spot any repeated patterns?
2 Clap or tap the rhythm whilst counting the pulse out loud.

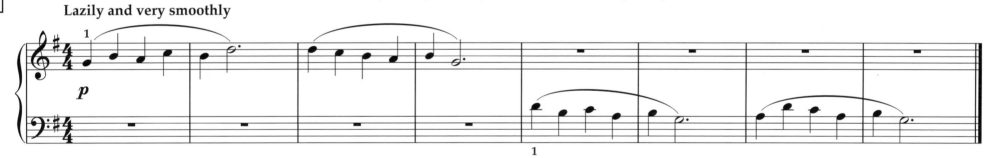

3

Dancing a habanera after a delicious paella

1 What is the similarity between bars 1–4 and bars 5–8?
2 Clap or tap the rhythm whilst counting the pulse out loud.

Grade 1 Stage 3

Can be used alongside
Improve your sight-reading!
Grade 1, Stage 4

1

Minuet in F (no. 99 from 100 Minuets in F K.625)

2

I'll have mine ... with onions

3

The tale of the old seafarer and the trout

Grade 1 **Stage 3**

CH

1

Minuet in F (no. 99 from 100 Minuets in F K.625)

1 What will you count? Clap or tap the rhythm whilst counting the pulse out loud.
2 What is the name of the second note in the second bar? Are there any more of these?

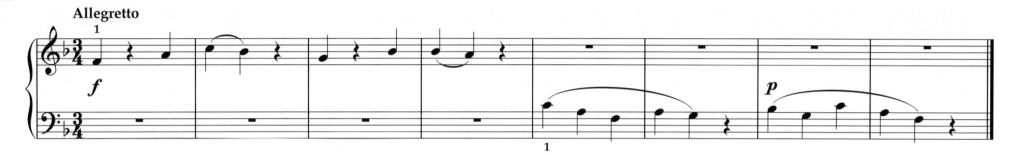

2

I'll have mine ... with onions

1 Clap or tap the rhythm whilst counting the pulse out loud.
2 How do bars 1–4 compare with bars 5–8?

3

The tale of the old seafarer and the trout

1 In which key is this piece? Play the scale (or microscale).
2 How do bars 1–4 differ from bars 5–8?

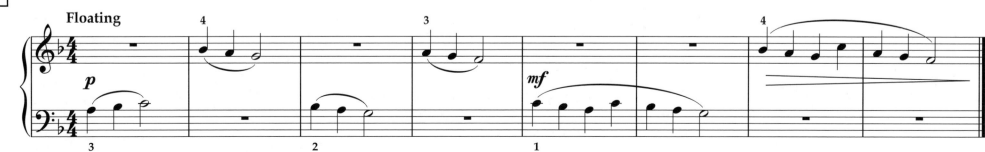

Can be used alongside
Improve your sight-reading!
Grade 1, Stage 5

Grade 1 **Stage 4**

1

All tied up

Heavily

2

You can count on me

Steadily

3

Secret agent TX9 saves the world

Explosively

Grade 1 Stage 4

CH

1 · All tied up

1 How many ties can you spot in this piece? Clap the rhythm, counting carefully.
2 What do you notice about each of the four phrases?

2 · You can count on me

1 In which key is this piece? Play the scale.
2 Are there any repeating patterns?

3 · Secret agent TX9 saves the world

1 How will you convey the character of this piece?
2 Clap or tap the rhythm then hear the rhythm in your head.

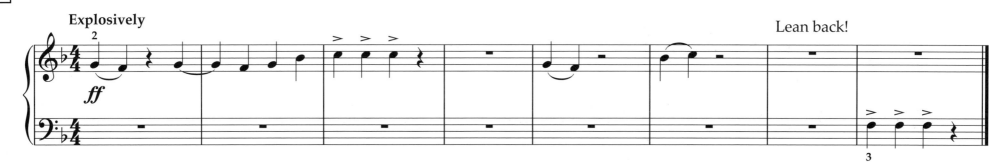

Can be used alongside
Improve your sight-reading!
Grade 1, Stage 6

Grade 1 **Stage 5**

1

The tune I play on my bagpipes before eating porridge

Strongly (with a bagpipe quality)

2

Taking the dog for a walk

Andante espressivo

3

Spending an afternoon at the movies

With a bucket of popcorn

Grade 1 **Stage 5**

1 ☐ **The tune I play on my bagpipes before eating porridge**

1 What do the curved lines indicate?
2 Are there any repeated patterns? Clap or tap the rhythm.

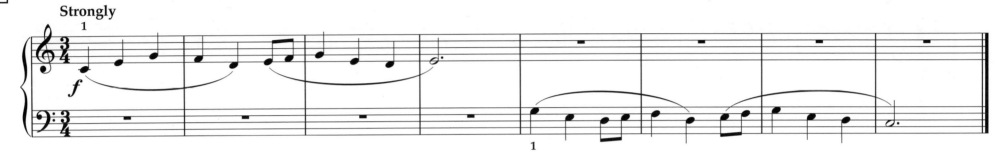

2 ☐ **Taking the dog for a walk**

1 In which key is this piece? Play the scale (or micro-scale).
2 How will you finger the big interval in bar 5?

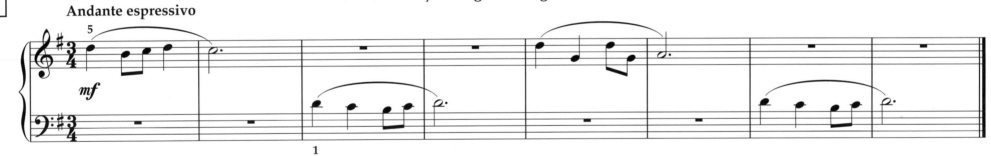

HT

3 ☐ **Spending an afternoon at the movies**

1 Are there any repeated patterns (rhythmic or melodic)?
2 Clap or tap the rhythm with one hand and the pulse with the other.

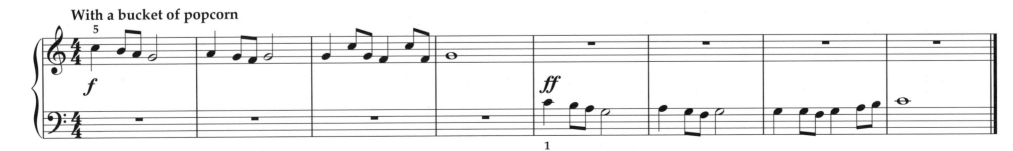

Grade 1 Stage 6

Can be used alongside
Improve your sight-reading!
Grade 1, Stage 6

1 **Secret agent TX9 goes to Russia**

Suspensefully

2 **Someone keeps interrupting**

Irritatedly

3 **TX9 on another case**

Secretly

Grade 1 Stage 6

1

Secret agent TX9 goes to Russia

1 What is the similarity between bars 1–2 and bars 3–4?
2 Clap or tap the rhythm with one hand and the pulse with the other. Then swap hands.

2

Someone keeps interrupting

1 How many times does the rhythm in bar 1 repeat? Clap or tap it.
2 In which key is this piece?

3

TX9 on another case

1 Can you spot the repeated patterns?
2 Play the first note, tap the pulse and try to hear the music in your head.

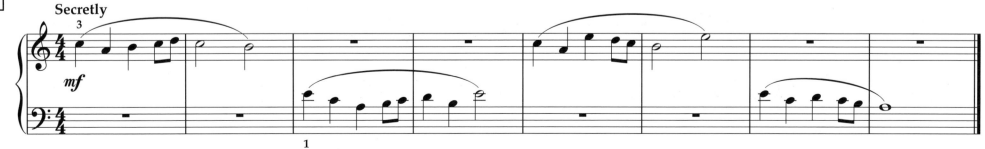

Grade 1 Stage 7

Can be used alongside
Improve your sight-reading!
Grade 1, Stage 7

1 | **Riding into the sunset**

2 | **Tuna crunch**

3 | **Uncle Bill tries dancing**

Grade 1 Stage 7

1 Riding into the sunset

1 How will you bring this piece to life?
2 Tap or clap the rhythm then, tapping the pulse, hear the rhythm in your head.

2 Tuna crunch

1 What is the interval in the first bar? Does this interval occur again later?
2 Tap or clap the rhythm with one hand and the pulse with the other. Then swap hands.

3 Uncle Bill tries dancing

1 How many beats are there in each bar? Are there any repeated patterns?
2 How will you give character to this piece?

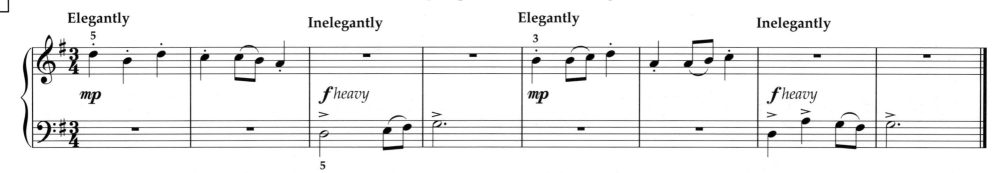

Grade 1 Stage 8

Can be used alongside
Improve your sight-reading!
Grade 1, Stage 8

1

At the court of King Henry VIII

Powerfully

2

Polite conversation

Andante

3

Strange goings on in the middle of the night

Darkly and mysteriously

Grade 1 Stage 8

D minor

1 **At the court of King Henry VIII**

1 What do the > mean?
2 How does the fourth phrase differ from the first three?

2 **Polite conversation**

1 In which key is this piece? Play the scale.
2 Tap the pulse and hear the rhythm in your head.

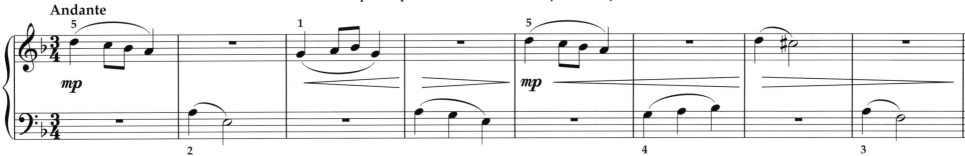

3 **Strange goings on in the middle of the night**

1 How will you add character to the piece?
2 Clap or tap the rhythm of the piece.

Can be used alongside
Improve your sight-reading!
Grade 1, Stage 9

Grade 1 Stage 9

1 Nearly the end of the book, so it must be time to beguine!

2 A trip to Moscow

3 At the circus

Grade 1 Stage 9

1 ☐

Nearly the end of the book, so it must be time to beguine!

1 There are lots of patterns here. How many can you find?
2 What is the key of this piece?

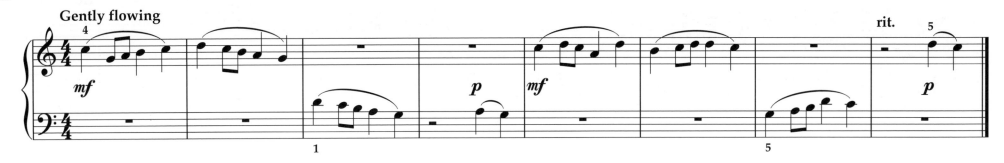

2 ☐

A trip to Moscow

1 In which key is this piece? How do you know that?
2 What is the marking between bars 1 and 2? Clap or tap the rhythm of the whole piece.

3 ☐

At the circus

1 How will you bring all the different markings to life?
2 Tap the pulse with one hand and the rhythm with the other. Swap hands.

To Diana, with thanks

© 2012 by Faber Music Ltd
This edition first published in 2012
Bloomsbury House 74–77 Great Russell Street London WC1B 3DA
Music processed by MacMusic
Cover and page design by Susan Clarke
Printed in England by Caligraving Ltd
All rights reserved

ISBN10: 0-571-52405-2
EAN13: 978-0-571-52405-1

To buy Faber Music publications or to find out about the full range of titles
available please contact your local music retailer or Faber Music sales enquiries:
Faber Music Ltd, Burnt Mill, Elizabeth Way, Harlow CM20 2HX
Tel: +44 (0) 1279 82 89 82   Fax: +44 (0) 1279 82 89 83
sales@fabermusic.com   fabermusic.com